The Parthian Stations

JOHN ASH was born in Manchester in 1948 and read English at the University of Birmingham. He lived for a year in Cyprus, and in Manchester between 1970 and 1985, before moving to New York. Since 1996 he has lived in Istanbul. His poetry has appeared in many publications including the *New Yorker*, the *New York Times*, the *Village Voice*, *Oasis*, *PN Review* and *Paris Review*. Two of his Carcanet collections, *The Goodbyes* (1982) and *Disbelief* (1987) were Poetry Book Society Choices. He has also written two books about Turkey, *A Byzantine Journey* and *Turkey: The Other Guide*.

T0159864

Also by John Ash from Carcanet

JOHN ASH

The Parthian Stations

CARCANET

First published in Great Britain in 2007 by
Carcanet Press Limited
Alliance House
Cross Street
Manchester M2 7AQ

Copyright © John Ash 2007

The right of John Ash to be identified as the author of this work
has been asserted by him in accordance with the
Copyright, Designs and Patents Act of 1988
All rights reserved

A CIP catalogue record for this book is available from the British Library
ISBN 978 1 85754 872 3

The publisher acknowledges financial assistance from Arts Council England

Typeset by XL Publishing Services, Tiverton
Printed and bound in England by SRP Ltd, Exeter

Contents

Part I

Part II

Part I

Apologia for an Earlier Book

In two months I wrote over sixty poems,
but that was because I had nothing better to do,
and, anyway, a lot of them were no good,
or so short they were mere gasps or sobs.
Others were about dumb subjects like soup
or plumbing. Still others came straight out of a bottle –
I really didn't know what I was saying,
or even if I was saying it, but I had no choice:

I had to stand by these damaged creatures,
who, without my folly, would have troubled no one.
They were doing their best, and somehow I liked them all –
the bad, the good, the short, the dumb, the drunk,
and as soon as they had died into their final form
I wanted them back in my head, where they belonged.
Damn, they were good company. Now what was I going to do?

Leaving New York I

I did not move from one
city to another.
I moved between different
versions of the same city.

What did I lose or gain? Friends,
an apartment with a beautiful ceiling,

blue views of the sea,
the outcry of gulls at sunrise.
Every street is the same
if you live on it.

Double Vision

We live in an antechamber of Asia,
in tall baroque or art nouveau buildings
without elevators, each one of us
a Janus or goddess of the crossroads,
amid magnificent but demoted
ambassadorial residences. Each morning,
we must choose which way to turn our faces,
The road westward leads into monotony,
and banal conceptions of luxury, deracinated...

This is not the capital or the capitol
(for what, in the end, is decided here?)
but a place of distances and perspectives –
Uccello's fallen swords aligned exactly
on the field of war. On clear winter days
the snows of Olympus dazzle us, and the sea
flashes like a polished shield. No choice,
no, none, for a vast expectancy awaits us.

Elements

The summoned neighbours
observed the phenomenon
with detached interest: smoke
was coming out of the woodwork.

The week before a small lake
appeared in the corridor.
Later a cascade fell on the bookcase
making arbitrary revisions to
the history of *Rome in the East*.

Despite the evidence, I can't believe
the elements are against me,
but remain watchful. Air, for example,
is beginning to cause trouble,
banging its fists on the windows.

As for the deceiving ground under us,
on that issue silence is the only option
if we are to escape madness, bodies falling.

Kubadabad (Arrival I)

The Russian prostitutes,
the Romanian prostitutes
harassed by police…

The Byzantine rotunda
converted to a mall…
The hotel on a noisy street where
the *asansör* was always *bozuk*…

The air-conditioning also failed.
I had to be taken to the hospital.
Diagnosis: severe dehydration.
Then, the day before a long bus journey,
I developed a haemorrhoid
the size of a butt-plug. What to do?

It was not a good beginning,
but it was at least that: a beginning.

I took the bus anyway, and squatted
for an hour in a cold bath in Afyon.
It helped, and on the following day
I stood by a lake under Mount Anamas
in the ruins of a sultan's summer palace,
as content with my life as I had ever been.

Stationary

I don't know where to go on to,
I don't know where to return to,
but I cannot remain stationary.

Although on certain days I may feel
like an engraved block, immovable,
I am not that. Never that...

Evening I

It would be ridiculous
to appear angry at things
I cannot alter. I don't want
to pull the dead from their graves.

How would it be if you
committed such an act?
The sun sinks anyway.

Drinking

A great Turkish poet,
or at least a great poet who lived
in Turkey (for he wrote in Persian)

once said: 'Being sober is not living'.
This has occasioned much commentary,
but it is my belief that he drank copiously,

albeit in a disciplined fashion,
and the wine he speaks of should not be
interpreted metaphorically,

though he may have felt that through it
he approached God. He was, after all,
a charming and honest person who wrote

affectionate letters to his daughter-in-law.
As to the distinctions Jew, Muslim,
Christian, they meant nothing to him.

In this book let him be praised.

Aunt Milka I

Once you were friend
to marvellous singers and artists,
and your scathing wit was famous.
How then did you sink
Into this fog, this limbo in which
nothing is distinct as you always were
like unrestrained laughter?

I neglected you, but it was out of fear.
You were a lost world still breathing,
still speaking in all the tongues of Babel:

'When I was young we always had Greek maids,
and Armenian friends, Jewish friends,
so of course I can speak Ladino. Spanish was easy.
All good families spoke French, and we were very good...'

And today the place you want to be
is where you cannot go, where no one can —
the old house with the maids amid
the buried gardens of the Asian shore.

Gratitude

On Wooden Castle Street
two blindmen walk by, arms
entwined, singing a folk song –

plaintive, nicely harmonised –
and they are greeted kindly:
coins drop into their open palms.

You know you're not in Manchester,
and you heave a profound sigh
of gratitude, but don't forget

the sorrow in the turnings
of the street, in dusty windows,
and fractured architraves over them.

Malediction I (Phil's Dick)

The detested boyfriend of a friend
nearly died of salmonella poisoning.
At once, I know it was all my fault.

When he recovered, relief
was mixed with deep disappointment,
for truly I had wished him out of life

like a virus or a tumour. He was in my home,
walking about it naked, and his whole body
was covered in pale fur, except his penis,

which bore a dark, purple stain
like a birthmark. Once, at breakfast,
he *showed it to me*. His mind was like it.

Mirror

It wasn't the riots or the wrecked stores,
the bad weather, the football,
or the new validation of greed –

no, the worst thing was returning
after several years to friends
who had become strangers with white hair,

and bellies that sagged
with unspoken sadness.

Were we becoming historical,
subjects for memory? For
a long time I looked in the mirror,

but found no revision
or renewal there. Behind me
the trees, the old trees clustered
in menacing conformations.

Four Quartets

The boxed set
of the complete quartets
of Zemlinsky sits before me

They are stupendously sad,
and formally perfect.
If they became my examples,

then all my vexations would become
a violent double fugue.

Everything it seems
ends in anger or lament.

Judith I

You were taken from us
when I was still very young –

exiled to a sanatorium in Wales,
a land I have hated ever since,
and, for you, what a desolation of boredom
it must have been. To occupy your time
you made soft toys. Mine was a duck
in a sailor-suit. I treasured it for years,
despite that fact that its too-long neck
went limp in a matter of weeks. You recovered,

and returned. You grew strong.
You married a good man, and had two sons,
but those years of absence made you hard to know.
I think I loved you. I assume that I did,
but could I have done without knowing you?

I remember standing in a rutted lane, looking through
a dense hedge, hoping to catch a glimpse of you
who were still too contagious for a closer approach.

Poem

People who don't believe
that a poem can kill you
don't know their history.

Usually, it is the poet
who is killed but the reader
should also be circumspect.

Book I

The idea was to move
decisively into new territory
where everything would be stark and clear,
a desert in moonlight –

some place beyond literature.
But if that is not where I am,
in a chair by the light of a lamp,
what exactly is this, this book?

Evening II

I have been thinking of the Maya
at the end of their Classic Period –
deserted cities, great causeways overgrown,
and of the terrible fate of 18 Rabbit, King
of Copan, who had grown overconfident.

The children are busy in the street,
the gas truck sings its stupid song,
and it is a pleasant evening in March.

Worry

Like my mother and father before me,
I am good at this. The trick is to worry
when everything is going right for you:

you are wealthy and in love, and your *château*
is surrounded by extensive formal gardens,
and you suddenly know this is too good to be true:

'Perhaps, unbeknownst to me,
my body already harbours a fatal disease,
or my lover secretly hates me, and even
now is plotting my downfall.'

It isn't likely of course,
but for heaven's sake use your imagination!
Think of what could surprise you
like a snowball in the back.

If you are fortunate you should worry.
Oedipus, you may recall, had a problem with this.

The Enigma of Jan Keetman

His mail arrives,
precisely addressed,
but he isn't here.

Is he Dutch or Danish?
Certainly he isn't German.
I think he has thin hair and stubble.

Sometimes the mailman despairs,
and leaves his orphaned letters
and packages at my door

like offerings to the god
of all that is foreign and infidel.

After all, we both have strange names,
and Jan is not so far from John.
I suspect that the mailman thinks

I am really this other person,
and, if he persists, I will give up
and finally confess my true identity.

But no, I must insist,
I am not, am not Jan Keetman.

Souvenir

On my desk there is a photograph
of Patsy, Helen, Peter and me
sitting around a table in the bar
of an expensive hotel (piano,
palm, framed calligraphy).

We are raising our glasses.
We look so happy I can't stand it.
Can it be so simple –
a sister, two friends and some booze?

And I think of the waiter
who must have taken the shot,
think of him smiling and deeply bored
by the duty to witness and record
the wealth and happiness of strangers.

Petersburg

For better or worse I am here
in the confusion of Istanbul.

I will not die in any
transparent city of art and song.

The walls will not shimmer.
I will simply mumble and pass away.

My Death I

The door was ajar.
Sunlight fell on the balcony,
casting shadows of leaves,
and the leaves themselves were falling.
A lake sobbed or sighed, an indifferent
music, and although the room was small
there was a feeling of immensity, of...

of *what* exactly? In truth, I had simply
changed hotel rooms and forgotten the fact.
(I was travelling. I was feverish.)
I had been dreaming of my death,
which approached with the imminence
and clarity of daybreak. Nearly blinding.

By now, I'm old enough
for this not to seem an affectation,
and there are times, my death, when
the only honest response to your absence
is a yawn like a canyon, long as a dynasty.

Morris I

We never knew how old you were.
It was one of Manhattan's deeper mysteries,
but sometimes you would say things like:

'Oh yes, Stravinsky's Symphony
in Three Movements. I was there with Ned.'
That was 1945. I started calculating

but never came to a conclusion.
You also wrote to Schoenberg
about a manuscript, and got a reply.

This was as good as encountering God,
or playing table-tennis with Gershwin.
But no, you cannot have done that.

Glass I

Oppressed by the angles of the buildings,
I reach for the glass and tell myself to stop.
Out of sight the winter sun is setting.

The glass is at my lips.

Smoking

My eyes were sore, were weeping
like those of a person in a Chinese poem
or a lyric by Lamartine...

There was something I hadn't seen:
smoke was blowing back from
the blue glass ashtray in front of me.

I moved it aside to a small,
Damascene table, but still the smoke
found its way back to my eyes.

The smoke, at least, was in love with me,
and believed that everything
should be a mystery for me, a veil

of sadness, but you, my tears,
are no more exceptional in this place
than a hot wind from the south.

Book II

Don't be fooled by
the apparent confidence of
the progression, the modulations...

I have no idea what I'm doing.
The words don't come, and they do
in the wrong order, and in great numbers.

This a vastation, or nothing.

Blank

I blank. I think of a shoeshine boy.
I remember the movie I saw on the bus,
in which the world ended, then did not.

Everything was reversed, confused
like a revolving rainstorm. Who are
the oppressed? The oppressors? Who
commits murder to enable freedom?

It's becoming difficult just
to walk down the street without
lamenting crones, and cart-loads
of cell-phones intervening,

but this is something I must do.
I mean walk. Remember
how that was? Simple as a song.

Malediction II (Arrival II)

I arrived with two bags,
and few books. I had given away
my rugs from Van, my jackets,
and the little art I possessed.

I knew perhaps six people,
and disliked half of them.
One was a witch, another
an embittered failure. They
were married in hell...

It took me some time
to understand this. Meanwhile,
they almost killed me. I was down,
they kicked me in the groin. Fuckers.

But I still live and breathe
with some freedom, while they,
I assume, are suffocating in ignorance
of their unique horribleness.
It would be a mercy to wish them dead.

Inclination

As I climb the steep hill past the music stores
for the thousandth time, and cats run for cover
under cars and the rain comes down and down
as it does in my home town, I think: 'My life is
horrible'. This idiocy goes on for perhaps a minute.

But still the sky doesn't clear.

Jesus

I met Jesus on the street,
and took him home. The sex was good.
In the morning, as he lay next to me,
he called his mother, who screamed abuse.
She lived in a village famous for kilims
with designs of birds and flowers.
I knew then that he was a outcast,
but not why. Later I found out
that he had killed someone in a knife fight.
This explained the net of scars on his belly,
the lightning shifts from charm to rage.

Isa, what did you want from me?
What could I have done to help and cure?
Like your homeland I failed you, and when you left,
for what I hope is the last time, you spat at me,
or rather made as if to spit, but did not.
This was a courtesy I had no right to expect.

Refusal

Now it is time
for other characters to speak out –
I have surely said enough by now –
so let me list their names.

No, I will not. It would take too long,
and it is not certain that they
would appreciate the gesture. I mean,
would you want to be in a poem like this?
It is a shambles. It has puked in its shoes.

Judith II

You were my sister, and you taught poetry,
so naturally I resented the fact that
you never once said a word pro or con

my poetry. It might have been better,
I like to think, if you had admitted
how much you disliked it, as I presume

you did. Of course, it is possible
that you were profoundly indifferent.
This came between us like a sheet of glass,

Sound-proofed. I was beginning to hope
things would change, when you were killed.
You were driving south along the narrow

Shropshire lanes, when, on a blind corner,
the car swerved out of control. A truck
was heading north loaded with gravel.

The dog survived, but you did not,
and now I complain merely because
your silence bruised my self-esteem.

Ararat

The lampshade is crooked.
The windows leak cold,
which settles in a pool
around my feet. I barely
understand a word
my neighbours say.

Ach, this damn language
in which the word for pain
is also the name of a town
in the remote east of the country,
where snow must now be falling.

I have nothing to regret, remembering
Ossia in exile dreaming of Ararat.

Evening III

It is a pleasant evening in March,
and there is no longer any need
to feel that you are being buried alive,
or there is less need. But this is a bad time –

a time for the breaking of teeth,
for nails to be pulled. The ballgame
was lost, the pyramid crashed. That
goes without saying. What humiliates

is the failure of the shamans,
and the idiocy of the crisis, its sheer
petulance, like pissing for no reason
on a bed in which an entire family must sleep.

Betrayal

No more words about the City
(It is becoming our idol
Ourselves the offerings).

No sad or celebratory images
Just photographs of function
(As if that were the real thing).

Photographs I can no longer take
Since some bastard stole my camera
At the exhausted end of a wedding party.

The marriage broke up. So nothing.
This is an aesthetic I will surely betray.

Aunt Milka II

Your house is empty.
The retarded boy no longer sits
in the gilded chair, his genitals
hanging out of his boxer shorts –
something which, then, you graciously
ignored, but now might not notice.

You said: 'The boy understands
a lot more than you'd think.'

His mother, your neighbour,
Stole your pearl earrings;
her daughter kept removing
by degrees your collection
of miniature, porcelain shoes.

And somewhere in the mid-distance
was Petkana, your wealthy sister,
spinning like a top under a huge red hat.

Urn

The map of my past life
is full of holes where homes should be,
and at the centre of the occasionally
inviting landscape stand three graves
I have determined never to visit.

Scatter me in the light
on the crowns of the olives.
I would not, for the world,
Award myself laurels.

Morris II

When Frank O'Hara was run down he was staying
at your summer place out on Water Island.
He drank too much, and was forever in love with
the wrong man, for which I will always admire him…

Frank, Larry, Joe, Ned, Virgil, Jane –
you knew everyone, were never dull,
and loved music with a passion: for you
poets and composers were equally collectable.
The invention of a shredding machine had made you
modestly wealthy, so you were not inclined
to worry overmuch, and once said, to my faint horror,
that the idea of being depressed made *you want to laugh*.

And you laughed. It was impossible not to forgive you.
You said this as a child might say to a grandmother:
'You're ugly'. Morris, you made me feel
that the horrible century was bearable, as
an overcrowded party was when half the people there
knew and loved you. I see you now setting off briskly
and slightly bow-legged for the endless Long Island beach,

wearing a battered cap against the sun,
a towel slung insouciantly over your shoulder.

Time and Again

Amongst my papers I discover
a postcard titled *The Day Slows Down
As It Progresses*. It shows
a street scene somewhere in India.

I have no idea who gave it to me,
and I hold the proposition to be wrong,
since the beginnings of my days
are slow as glaciers. It is only later

that an accumulation of mostly
trivial incidents faintly suggests
the idea of forward motion, rivulet
of dust, but moving towards what?

I can't say, but as I undress
I am happy to have vanquished
the appalling vacancy of sluggard hours
and iterative seconds clicking like beads.

Short Poems I

I always wanted to write short poems
but never could. Often I would write five lines

and say to myself with hope in my heart:
'There, it's done. I have said everything,

and how sheerly *pithy* it is!' But soon
the poem would grow restless, squirming

in its too-tight sailor suit, demanding
long pants, cigarettes and alcohol.

For hours, for a day I held out,
issuing stern refusals, turning my back

to the mirror, the window, the terrace,
but how could I deny my child anything?

Great yearning eyes, frail bones
undid me, and, in no time five grew tenfold.

Arrival III (Departure)

A divided sky above the great dome…
The rain that had pounded the vines
and the fire-escape all night,

moving off towards the unglimpsed
sea called Black… At the hotel,
the pillows were like landfill.

We didn't care. We had arrived,
and now could depart in fair weather
into what was entirely unknown to us.

Grinning boys waved the boat off
with fishing lines. Between the City
and the islands a dolphin broke surface.

What was it that we were about to find,
and what would we fail to find
on disembarking in blue Bithynia?

To all appearances unbruised,
innocence had been restored to us
like a pearl lost in the back of a taxi.

Kamchatka

– geologically speaking
the most unstable part of the earth's crust.
Things aren't too much better here,
and there are the added disadvantages
of traffic and shoeshine boys. Be that as it may…

there is no explanation for it,
but today I am convinced that I have
always longed to visit the peninsula
of Kamchatka, to see its icy lakes,
its smoking mountains and quivering stones,

At least now I am a little nearer.

Vinegar

To be exiled to Prote
or Prinkipo
cannot have been so bad.

The climate must have been
just as mild, the roses and pines
as lovely. Trotsky
survived it easily
in an elegant house.

It cannot have been so bad,
provided, that is,
you were allowed to keep
your eyes. O
the polished bowl,
the boiling vinegar!

Hero I

There is war in Afghanistan.
To signal my disapproval
I plan to visit Beirut soon.
My god, what a hero!

Samarkand

In Merv only 400
craftsmen were left alive
out of a population
of one hundred thousand...

In Herat, after an
injudicious revolt,
everyone was killed.

As to the fabulous city
of Afrasiab, which it took
a day to cross on horseback,

it was so completely destroyed
that its name was lost ever after
to travellers, cartographers.

But calm yourself,
it found refuge in a great poem –

obviously not this one.

Short Poems II

Why are short poems sad
even when they evoke good weather
and agreeable hours spent loafing in cafés?

There is a mystery.
There is something locked away,
something unsaid.
And the unsaid becomes a circle
of monuments with eyes
looking in towards the sprig
or nosegay of the poem,

crushed but defiant,
in its absolute refusal to acknowledge
the great news of the world. Also,

it should be short enough to fit
in chiselled letters on a tombstone
of only modest size, addressing itself
to the smallest shudders of a cypress.

Tell me again,
why are short poems sad?

Junk

Is there anyone whose telephone cord
doesn't get tangled? Yes,
I have seen them in ads. They recline
on sofas, or sit laughing at their desks...

Out there dust rises in the vicinity
of towns named for Alexander,
and junk food in yellow packages
drops into the middle of a perfectly level,
dessicated plain where leaves fall
from the poplars with a brassy sound.

The manuscripts are gone, and the immense statues.
It makes no sense, but they of the untangled cords,
must know better: they are so attractive,
so bland like bed-linen. Only we do not,
and feel that our lives, our judgements
have been taken from us like a sister –

Arachosia unremembered...

Malediction III

When Randy Newman wrote the line
'Short people ain't got no reason to live'
he must have had you in mind.

Bad drunk, but just as crazy off the sauce
as on, you can't wait to see my friend,
your partner, nodding, helpless in a wheelchair.

Contemptible runt, you have intelligence enough
to know his value, and you must always
have something or someone of great value

at your mercy. What you can't be you must ruin.
May your asshole shrivel and close over. That way
you will be full to your skull with what you are.

Ruin

A clanking swarm of bottles.
Lemon rind. A chicken wing
in the mouth of a cat. The stench
in the hallway. Continuous
partial breakdown in the centre
(pushed to the edge) in the suburbs
(crowding in) in the hidden heart
of Lesser Asia foul black streams
at the bottom of verdant ravines –

excrement (fresh,
human) in the castle gate.

Cursed

Nearly twenty years after the event
you could still see the bullet-holes
and shell-holes in the walls of the houses.

Nothing had been done to restore
the little that had been left standing,
or rebuild in the old style the banded walls

of limestone and basalt. And in this
was a malign intent. It was all
unforgiven, unforgivable on all sides.

Out of crushed bones and corrupted
flesh a white, pyramidal hotel
rose in balconied stages. Cursed.

Short, Bad Imitation

I am in competition
with a thirteenth-century master,

but, no, I'm not. I loathe the very
idea. Does life last forever

that I can waste it? But I still
I gaze on the face of the Friend

I have never encountered.
He talks of birds, of stars and roses

On these subjects I remain silent.

Aunt Milka III

Your adored nephew's long letter
went astray, or so I think he said.
But it is quite possible I dreamt this.

These days I'm dreaming so lucidly,
I confuse it with memory. You could say
we're in the same boat oneirically speaking

The phone call wasn't much help either.
The hospital was La Paix, not Pasteur.
At least both were French. Once, this
would have amused you. You were there,

asleep on your side, but the walls were bare.
Where were the landscape paintings,
the framed photographs of the elegant Kebir,

your husband, whose death you had forgotten?
As to that boat, I dreamt it was crossing
Lake Iznik on a day of perfect calm.

You leant over the side, and your necklace,
which had been catching the light,
came unclasped, sinking swiftly out of sight.

Shard (Glass II)

A writer I know has the inveterate habit
of confusing the words 'shard' and 'sherd',
but the difference is crucial. The first
refers to glass the second to clay,
and today, I'm afraid, is a day of sherds
already crushed underfoot. So it is

that I remember the cloud-coloured neck
of a Roman tear-bottle I found at Salamis.

Morris III

Now I have a postcard of you, Morris.
You look handsome and fiendishly gay
(in both senses of the term), but recently

you died, which is the last thing
I ever thought you would do.

Leaving New York II

When I left Manhattan I said in explanation:
'I want to live somewhere where there are muezzins!'
The desire was real enough, but why did it exist?

It may have been the desire to shuck responsibility,
to imagine I was not Western, not Christian and free.
But I was free, and am. So why does death seem near?

Surabaya

I can't bear the way I bear things
that are clearly unbearable.

For sure, the tears come, and I take
to my bed and sleep until noon,

but then I get up, stuff the sheets
(the expensive sheets from New York)

into the machine and am somehow
charmed by its slow revolutions.

For sure, *du hast kein herz, Johnny.*

Terrorist (Hero II)

Instead of Beirut, I went to Syria.
It was less trouble, and, in moral terms,
what was the difference? In the blind eyes
of the imperium this too was a pariah.

And how pleasant it was
to renew acquaintances in the bar
of the Baron Hotel, to talk of Dame Freya
and the beauty of the ruined towns.

It was the end of Ramadan and the souks
were closed, which made the place feel wintry,
and there was no trace of Jemal,
the helplessly over-emotional barman

who once said to me in the hours before dawn:
'I have eight children. I work two jobs.
I get so tired, I drink too much. I go home.
My wife wants to make love. I don't know what
I am doing. We have more babies!…'

Was it out of courtesy or cowardice
that I did not ask where he had gone? Nothing
was said. I hoped earnestly that he was happy,
that there were no more babies, that he still made love.

Recess

In Adana a drum was beating.
In Haleb the dog barked all day.
In Antioch the concierge was snoring.
In Hama the waterwheels had stopped –

the Orontes,
the Rebellious One,
reduced to a sluggish sewer.

At Khirab Shems
a dark, handsome man danced
above the arches of a church.

I was possessed by
a contradictory nostalgia
for things I had never known,
for emptiness: the recesses of Bamiyan.

Brad

I sometimes wonder
if the many American males
called Brad (Gooch, Pitt, Morrow)
are aware that their name is also
the name of the largest Byzantine town
in northern Syria, and if they were
would it materially alter the way
they perceived themselves? For now,

that flat monosyllable would be
associated with great architecture
and the abandonment, many centuries
ago, of vineyards and olive groves.

I doubt it, but would like not to,
since I have spent days amid stony hills
trying to find you but failed utterly, O Brad!

I will not give up. You will be *mine* I tell you.

Names

When travelling in Turkey
I like to translate the names
of the places I pass through.

I am always touched
by the number of them
that are called Yeşilköy,

which means Green Village,
for the people in these parts
have a great love of trees,

and of pure water,
which they will gather
at wayside fountains

miles from any habitation.
But there are surely names
that have no meaning,

or meanings that are long lost –
stone pomegranate, blood of the light…
Yet they keep a resonance,

an oblique music
that can carry us very far away
from ourselves like a passion.

Next

So where have we come to,
and what might be our destination,
presuming it will go beyond this

as it is? I forget everything
you told me last night at the party.
Was it important? Probably...

It has been raining for two months.
My thoughts are as soaked as my shoes.
Snow is expected. I'm at a loss

to know which border I must cross next.
Must I once again take leave of everything –
Books, rugs, shirts, music, paintings,

and you the friends without whom
I feel I cannot live, but will
if so consigned. I have no wife.

My Death II

I have outlived to an absurd degree
so many of the poets I admire,
and to what end? There are

salad vegetables I would regard
with more respect (if correctly dressed)
than certain persons I've encountered.

in the course of days that seemed
only a poor means of digesting time.

Lover

Winter is ending,
but the dark still comes
too early. And at this time,
after a strong drink or two,

I would like to address a lover
of the kind one finds in books
I would compare the page
to snow, or the purity of my desires,

but then would break off in lines
of dots, or blurs like sleet,
for it truly isn't cold enough
for snow. Today, for example,

somewhere from a taxi
in an anonymous suburb I saw
an almond tree in flower. Besides,

these longings are derived from a poem
written in another, colder country,
in another century. Are and are not.

Passion

is an absolute necessity.
Almost any object (or subject)
will do, provided it is obscure enough,
so that it remain *yours*,
and you can possess it completely
as people once talked of possessing a woman.

We can no longer say this without rebuke,
which is perhaps a pity, since it is a powerful term
and meant a great deal to many people for many years,
but, yes, surely it is a loathsome phrase.

But to be consumed by a passion –
well – that is everything.
An idea of formidable abstraction?
A sleeve? Sassanian architecture?

It must all be held in possibility –
that broad chamber unhung
by drapes of circumstance.

Anna / Marthe

It must be sad I suppose
that I don't know what poets mean
by the 'love' they apostrophise so
incessantly. I am reminded of the type-
writer in Satie's *Parade*. Even if

I placed Anna Akhmatova's
riding-crop and gloves under
a powerful microscope the chance is
I still wouldn't get it. She must
have had better things to do than ask

'Why did you go?' while inhaling
'the lindens' sweet scent'. In fact,
the scent of lindens is oppressive.
They ooze and are sticky. Lust

I know, and infatuation. They are things
to get over like a gate or a fence
until you come to rest, as Bonnard did,
in a garden close to the Mediterranean,

with a wife who lived like Danaë
in a bathroom washed with gold.

Luxury

The worst will happen or it won't,
here or in the Hindu Kush. Nothing,
I suppose, can alter this condition
except what is lacking: money or water.

Small victories help. At the border post
the bus ran away with the beautiful coat
I had inherited from my father. I *got it back*,

and as I plunged my arms into its wide sleeves,
was overwhelmed by a sense of luxury:
there was nothing I could do, and nothing
I couldn't. Nothing, such a wide country.

Things

I am trying to tell you about these things —
these names, and feelings, and places.
They may be of no interest to you,
and they don't seem to help much,
but I think they are real in ways

we can't imagine like gloves
in a coat pocket or a thorn in a hem.
No less so when they exist
in no observable dimension.

Book III

It is becoming increasingly
obvious that I did not write you.
This would explain a lot. But who,
in that case, can be held responsible?

On whose doorstep should
the dead child be set down?

Backwards

Not wanting to be part of a crowd,
I made my farewells to the twentieth century
some years before it ended,
but it occurs to me that I said and did
nothing to greet the new century apart from
getting drunk on the appropriate night.

This is partly a matter of preference –
for a farewell is an entire landscape with tombs
and a sunset, while a greeting is merely
a door opening onto an uncertain hallway.
Even so, I would like to correct the omission:

'So here you are twenty-first century,
and perhaps surprisingly, I am here too.
It is only the end of your second year,
but already you are beginning to look old,
and there are good reasons for wishing
you would vanish like an epidemic
without further, monstrous repetitions.'

This, of course, is not what I meant to say.

Judith III

What emerged after your death
astonished us –
the expensive jewellery, the vast
and comprehensive collection of lingerie –

the silks, the lace, the linens...
We had difficulty giving it all away.
We were open-mouthed. We knew
you loved your life, but not that you had

such a taste for luxury. Then I understood
that you were truly my sister. Sad girls,
your students, sang at your requiem.

Possible

If we are dying, and we are,
if the wars continue,
albeit on somewhat altered terms,
and our cities are collapsing,
then it's best to make the most of it –

drink wine, some coffee,
take pleasure in conversation.

No more than this: only
philosophies of the possible.

Book IV

Why did it take me so long?
I realise now that you have many authors,
some of whom don't speak a word of English;
some are beautiful young women: others
rode in carriages through the perfumed nights
of Ch'ang-an: one may even have been a bishop
who wrote obscure commentaries on Homer.

Inevitably it saddens me to reflect
that so many of you are no longer living.

Leaving New York III

Here the call to prayer isn't looked on as music,
but what else can it be, as it hovers over the city
like a swarm of birds or benign insects singing

in praise of the sky, eternal and temporal
divinity who, too evidently, is not with us?
In the hour before dawn the verse grows by one line,

not otherwise heard, urging the supremacy
of prayer over sleep. But what kind of salvation
would it be that broke us from our dreams?

In New York there are many churches,
but I do not remember their bells.

My Death III

I think of you as a calm businessman
with a prospectus and a taste for music
that is at once witty and dignified.

Certainly, there is nothing about you
that pertains to the Gothic,
which the Victorians ruined for all time –

Blackened walls
Of childhood O Manchester...

In the end, it couldn't be so bad
to be part of a landscape –
hewn stone sunning itself, ash
under a tree of the same name,

but there are still some reasons
for delay, if that is possible.
My death be patient.

Leaving New York IV

I never left. I am still leaving.
I never arrived. I am still arriving.

I talk. I move around. I buy
books and music. It is never enough.

I forget. I am forgotten.
Even time abandons me –

far out on my own periphery,
when *the idea was to be at the centre of things*,

and this, of course, is a line
I wrote some twenty years ago.
Everything returns in time
to the place that gave it birth,
and leaving answers no questions.

Empire

All my life I have been watching
empires decline, and disperse like chaff,

(or so it now occurs to me)
and have observed the process without
too much regret, since it appears

to be as unstoppable as winter cold –
the Franks crossing the frozen Rhine
without either animosity or understanding –

or the decay of knowledge, the onset of the dark.
We are there, and hapless. Who, in all of this,
could you ask to intercede like a god or a mother?

Auguries

The auguries, the inaugurations
proceed at vast expense, banquet after banquet.
A fire of the mind is invoked, and this is what
we must live with as the century raises itself
on crippled limbs to proclaim victory.
Neither Alexander nor Trajan combined
such arrogance with ignorance
but, in the end, what difference does it make?
Persepolis burned, and Fallujah is emptied.

God

The great wave washed over
the Swedes and Sri Lankans equally,
but why has God been brought into the equation?
His sublime indifference was argued
centuries ago by Epicurus, and I, for one,
am deeply convinced, but would go further.
And perhaps a little compassion is in order:
after all, the Great Lummox resides in heaven,
which is not exactly the most down-home
neighbourhood. So what would He know?

Glass III

Once, someone dropped a brick on my head.
The sound was like that. Then, a second later,
the windows blew out. I didn't know
what was happening. Who could have?
Friends were wandering in the square,
dazed, but unbloodied. We sat in the café
(what else was there for us to do?)
as a tall plume of smoke rose towards
the clear September sky. The grapes were dying
on the trellised vine above us, and the smoke...
the smoke was the colour of saffron. Beautiful –

Scythopolis

The wall goes up, its circuit
the image of insanity. The olive groves
are cut down, the houses levelled.
No need to mention the death of children,
this alone is crime enough.
Without foresight or memory, we have
entered the Second Century of the Wolf.

Say nothing or risk calumny.
The processional way leads
to the obliterated temple,
and monuments of unknown purpose.

Gone

James had the horrors,
and ended up in a secure place
with gardens and a chimney
like a Roman column; Sarp,
the sad carpenter, lost his mind;
the doors of a nursing home closed on Milka;
a soprano sang in memory of Morris,

and, on the last afternoon of the year,
Ömer called in quenched tones
to say that his beloved mother had died.
Would I come to the funeral? Of course I would.
The hearse was green with dull silver swags,

and a bad year gone,
unreturnable as wine bottles.

Short Poems III

I have enjoyed your company,
although it is true that some of you
could have been shorter, and it is
perhaps a pity that so many of you
had to allude to war and death.

I assure you this was not my intention.
I wanted you to have a good time,
but the laws intervened: I could not,
after all, misrepresent life.

Orhan Veli was a poet who wrote
many very fine, very short poems,
but his life was also short: one night
he fell into a ditch, and, a little later, died.

In one of his poems he wrote:
'It isn't easy to leave this world.'
The corpse's watch is still ticking.

Part II

Against Symbolism

In Manhattan there are the towers,
and the depths between the towers. To call
the first phallic or the second vaginal

would be absurd. Nothing, in the end,
can be a symbol of anything beyond itself –
a tall tower is a tower and tall, no more,
else we would go mad associatively.

We do not. We understand that
the silhouette we have built is beautiful,
and contains us against an evening sky –
erect, open, unhaunted by any god...

Yet there is a wound here, and the smoke
of a hatred that must be disowned. Say,
that you are looking south from your roof.
It is night, and those great honeycombs of light

are gone. Calm yourself. Nothing is required
except patience and knowledge. It will all pass
like a train of ghosts, as the empire declines
in ignorance of its condition like a syphilitic.

But how lovely the towerless night is
as we go down, as they go down with
their appalling gods, as all goes down.

The Reconstructions

It has been many years in preparation,
but the concert will have to be postponed.
The reconstructions have been challenged.
They are all 'merely conjectural',
'Orphic approximations', etcetera…

Reluctantly we turn our attention
back to the instruments as depicted
on vases, in frescoes and mosaics. We have
some obscure notations, but how are these
to be converted into sounds proper to
Aeschylus or the Byzantine court?

But Anatolia is a continuum,
and perhaps it is only necessary to listen
more acutely to what can still be heard –
the blind fiddler in the theatre, where springs
break from the rock, plunging down
toward Xanthos, crossing, reordering
the tracks we can follow. And Beethoven,
in his last years, sometimes wrote adagios
in the modes of Phrygia and Lydia,

and there are places where we hear nothing
beyond a cold sussuration in tall stands of pines,
but still the music wells up inside us –

clear, terrible and calm –
and we can't open our mouths.

The orders have been cancelled (Doric,
Ionic, Corinthian). The concert will be silent.
The music will be the music of its place.

The Parthian Stations

1

In battle they unfurled scarlet, silk banners,
the better to dazzle their enemies.
They favoured magnificent moustaches,
voluminous pants, and the lavish application
of rouge and kohl. Superb horsemen
and archers, they menaced Antioch,
but founded many cities of their own,
all of them forgotten, as are they, hidden under
absurd approximations of their names.

Perhaps what most impugns them in our eyes
is the nonchalance with which they thwarted
the vainglorious designs of their western rivals:
thus, at Carrhae, Crassus came to grief,
and the standards were seized by a prince of Suren,
whose courage and beauty Plutarch salutes.

In architecture they made great innovations,
in sculpture also, but have received small credit,
being mere nomads, aliens, barbarians,
who yet had a taste for Greek theatre –
yes, beyond Zagros, even beyond Zagros…

2

Although he lived far from the Greek lands,
like so many who were drawn eastwards
in Alexander's wake, Isodoros of Charax
must surely have been conscious of his ancestry –

Greek through and through. I see him
sitting in sight of the crowded waterways
of Basra, composing with infinite care,
his description of the towns and way-stations
extending along the royal road
from the palm groves of the twin-rivers
to Kandahar, which he called, resoundingly,

Alexandria ad Arachosia. But how
accurate was his knowledge of these places?
How shallow, how dry, and an uninformative his account
now appears, and who now knows these names,
or cares for what they must once have meant?

Seleucia ad Tigris, Ctesiphon –
the people dying in their thousands,
corpses uncounted, under the rubble.

Hotel Seferis

The gardens with the towering pines,
the secret courtyards with the lemon trees –
these had not been burnt,
and under the arches of the agora
water still gushed from a nymphaion,
dispersing into curving channels
that vanished under the new city
of mirrored high-rises and storied car-parks.

Along a street of vines
I stumbled on the emptied Jewish quarter:
four locked doors of synagogues
in an area no larger than a garden.

Open city 1922...

The regular footfalls of the gendarmes
were no longer heard at night,
and the citizens shivered behind
high walls that could not protect them.

Lice-infested, lice-like, half-starved,
a rabble of soldiery fled headlong westwards.
Their ships left no trace amid
the scatter of islands beyond Erythrae.

Then, at an hour no one can agree upon,
flames began to creep through the streets,
the gardens, the churches and the schools,
and soon, on the narrow quayside,
voices rose in a fugue of horror, drifting out
to the warships of Europe and America,
lying at anchor in the bay.

On their immaculate decks
phonographs crackled into life
playing arias and waltzes
to accompany the dinner parties,
for the screams of the dying
or the merely terrified do little

to further the designs of diplomacy.
A wall of fire advanced towards the sea.

From the citadel,
where imperturbable women
still wove carpets
according to the old patterns,
I saw it all, and understood nothing.
How is understanding possible
in a world reduced to an endless hotel?
We are left with echoes in corridors,
with bathroom mirrors, with illusions like Helen.

At the conference, the charming professor
began to speak of houses by the sea –
their joys and sorrows,
their bitterness when stripped bare.
She said: 'I don't know much about houses',
but the moderator cut her short,

as if he feared we might perceive
something hidden under the words –
a carved stone, a jar – and be moved
to the point of a sharp, salt clarity.

But she had already said enough,
and next day we set out along the peninsula,
in the track of agonised retreats,
history burning like the Alexandrian library,
looking for the one house amid so many –
the house of 'coloured shutters and shining doors',

In Urla we looked in the wrong quarter.
A clear stream divided the town: on one side
was a mosque with antique columns;
opposite were the painted houses of the Greeks,
but not *his* house, nor the garden where
he had played with 'tassels of the sun'.

Seferis, Seferiades, Seferhisar…
The dictionary told me that *sefer* in Turkish
meant *journey, voyage, state of war, time, occurrence.*
This, at least, seemed close to the truth of his life.

Then, one of us remembered
that the professor had mentioned
the word *skala*, which we knew meant
port or harbour, deriving from Italian,
emerging in Turkish as *iskele*. So
we followed the trace of the word along
a beautiful, straight road, vaulted by pines.

Winter storms had damaged the quays,
and here was Clazomenae, a city as old as Troy,
famed for sarcophagi made of terracotta,
decorated with scenes of mythical contest,
so precious and so fragile that, during the years
of war, the soldiers (young, half-crazed
with victory or defeat) could not resist
the urge to smash them into pieces.

Who is not exiled? Who does not lack a home?
Why do fires still burn that were started a century ago?

The arcade seemed about to collapse into the bay.
Fallen plaster covered the paving-stones.
It was all familiar as paintings by De Chirico,
and I expected, at any moment, to meet someone I knew –

someone who had stepped out of history,
someone who had been old, but had grown young again.

A light breeze fluttered the table-cloths.
I was among friends, yet irritable,
possessed by something close to dread,
and looking at a napkin or the horizon
saw statues with mutilated limbs
stumbling out of the museum.

But I continued to eat, to drink, to look at the sea.

It was at the last minute, after we had bought
the herbs and the olive oil, that we saw the sign
declaring in discreet, gold letters *Yorgos Seferis Otel.*
The walls were thick, built of dark stone.
The rooms were also dark, and encumbered –
each piece of furniture the tomb of something,
but why had I expected colours, views and balconies?

Perhaps my reading had been too literal.
I backed away from the gloom of the stairwell
As if rebuffed, and thought of what had escaped –

of the courtyard with the lemon tree
and the fountain, where Eleftheria was singing.

The Bathers

1

It would be apt if it were true,
but Renée didn't drown herself
in a bathtub. Nor did you discover
her corpse. She was many miles from you,

and had ideas of her own. Filling her bed
with white lilacs, she lay down among them,
and applied a small revolver to her head.

Under Marthe's orders you destroyed
your portraits of her, except for one,
which you concealed for over twenty years,

only resuming when Marthe herself
was dead. Broad-faced, large-eyed,
Renée smiles towards us, untroubled,
her head resting on her right hand.

In the revision, it is the gold of her
tousled hair that takes complete possession
of the image, invading the bowl of fruit
that rests on a cloth striped with more

tawny gold. And, against all logic,
the very ground of the garden is also gold.
For Renée remembered, even the dirt
under her feet must be a glory.

It is all tranquil radiance, until
we notice a dark area in the lower,
right-hand corner, and recognise,
with something like a shiver,

Marthe's unsmiling profile, her dull,
severely cropped hair. It is as if Night
were regarding Day, consumed with envy.

O Marthe, muse and monster –
you are always there, in the violet
shadows of the room, and the tablecloth

is a paradise of colours tilted
violently against our eyes. Even when
you are almost illegible, bending down

to the ubiquitous, small, black dog,
you are there, eluding us. Even
your name was an invention. Of

your family or origins nothing is known –
your every glance and gesture steeped
in oblivion. The sea or the garden might

blaze like a peacock's fan behind you,
but under them was the unworked canvas.
You took his name, but sometimes called yourself

Solange. It was an attempt at distance,
when really there was none. Perhaps he
became you, taking your regnal place

in the dead waters of the bath. Or
you became him, and the transference
occurred between walls soaked in violet,

in lilac, red, gold and orange-gold –
colours remembered through the mist
of an intolerable longing…

No empress was ever so attended.

There was nothing you could do to stop
your sickness, the incursions of light,
his constant enquiry into your nature,

but it is possible that you saw this
as love, as devotion. Years after
you had died at the age of seventy-three,

he still painted you as young, lissom,
small-breasted, as the girl he had first
encountered, stepping off a tram in Paris,

3

Now, it is you to whom we must turn
(and your image to which you turned)
old, alone, at the end of a war,

deprived of lover, invalid, wife,
you materialise in blurred
formations in the bathroom mirror

wearing the mask of a Japanese ghost,
and it is surely you who peers out at us
from the long, desolate face of a circus horse —

its solid, black eyes admitting no light.
You saw death coming, but didn't hurry
the marriage. You were also *The Boxer* —

skinny arms, puny fists flailing,
and feinting towards the glass above
a shelf crowded with those ordinary

objects that were your hope,
and redemption. Head bloodied,
eyes nearly sightless, you still saw

with joy the stoppered bottles, the jars
the unguents, powders, soaps and perfumes
she had left behind. These were a treasure,

not easily earned, but yours
like that almond tree in flower
you painted in your last days —

the intense indigo
of the Mediterranean sky
penetrating, like eyes,
the white of the blossoms.

From your deathbed you continued
to effect alterations on the ground,
pained to discover you hadn't lied enough.

Your nephew, Charles, applied
the necessary, transfiguring gold,
and at last on darkness the dark eyes
closed, brimming with the memory of colour.